Deep Calling Deep

Deep Calling Deep

POETRY COLLECTION

Sherri Stevens

Library of Congress Control Number: 2021908813

HARDBACK: 978-1-955347-36-5
PAPERBACK: 978-1-955347-35-8
EBOOK: 978-1-955347-37-2

Ordering Information:

For orders and inquiries, please contact:
1-888-404-1388
www.goldtouchpress.com
book.orders@goldtouchpress.com

Printed in the United States of America

To all those who have ever felt like they were
drowning in a deep sea of pain and loss.

"Surely the hand of The Lord is not too short to save,
nor His ear too dull to hear." – Isaiah 59:1

Contents

Introduction

Within all of our hearts is a deep longing – an inconsolable cry for a passion we sense is missing. In the roar of our waterfalls, we hear a Voice, *Deep Calling Deep*. It is the Voice of our First Love arousing in us a profound yearning for ecstasy, artistry, and adventure with Him.

This collection of poems describes the very raw and honest spectrum of my faith-journey. Initially, I was reluctant to share the dark side of my many years wrestling with God. I thought it would be dishonoring to God, and I didn't want to do that. However, after much prayer and contemplation, I concluded that the Bible is very inclusive of honest struggles and heartfelt lamentations of suffering souls. Because I believe God invites and honors such authentic grappling of our faith, I have written this collection of poems to share with others mosaics of my misery as well as kaleidoscopes of my conquests through Christ.

Ironically, it was during my darkest years that I found the Book of Job to offer me the most comfort. Job's account revealed an unapologetic underbelly of the kind of honest struggle I could relate to. Other stories I had come across that were all wrapped up in their neatly tied bows didn't fit my pain paradigm. At best, they were irrelevant and irritating. At worst, they were incendiary and mocking. Plus, I felt like such saccharine storytellers had little to no "street cred" to speak into my life about real pain and heartache. I would hear my heart screaming, "SERIOUSLY? You call that pain?" Hence, the reason I was inspired to write *Deep Calling Deep*, and not *Shallow Calling Shallow*.

Darkness gives dimension. Troubles give texture to a tapestry. *Deep Calling Deep* is a very textured tapestry - the good, the bad, and the ugly. But I would rather have an "ugly win" than a "pretty loss," and I believe that is the very essence of this book.

I have found that if the pain is not transformed, it will be transferred. Writing this book has helped transform me. My mess became my message. Although many loose and knotted threads still remain dangling from the underbelly of my tapestry, I have attempted to weave my words into a handicraft of healing, both for myself and hopefully others.

"He comforts us in all our troubles so that we can comfort others. When they are troubled, we will be able to give them the same comfort God has given us" - 2 Corinthians 1:4

Preface

Scuba diving, as with love, can be rapturous but risky. Trained scuba divers understand a condition called nitrogen narcosis, also known as the Martini Effect because the diver feels as if he has drunk a martini on an empty stomach – the calculation is one martini for every additional fifty feet of depth.

Nitrogen from a diver's tank increases in pressure as a diver descends. When the body is at high pressure, nitrogen gas saturates the blood and tissues. The amount of extra nitrogen dissolved in the body's tissues is directly related to the depth (pressure) to which the diver dives and the amount of time he spends underwater. The problem, however, is not with the descent but the ascent.

When the diver ascends after a dive, the extra nitrogen is released from his tissues and back into the blood. If he ascends slowly enough, his lungs can remove this excess gas by exhaling it. If he ascends too quickly or has too much nitrogen dissolved in his tissues, bubbles will form in his blood, producing a manifestation of decompression sickness known as the bends. The deeper a diver descends, the slower he or she must ascend and/or make intermittent stops on the way up (called "decompression stops") to avoid the bends.

To a certain extent, deep love is like deep-sea diving – both can be euphoric and intoxicating. But when the bond of deep love is broken, the result can be devastatingly painful and the source of much grief. Often, well-meaning people attempt to rush our "resurfacing" too quickly back from the depths of a heartbreaking loss or trauma. When this happens, a state of "emotional bends" occurs. It is my hope that *Deep Calling Deep* would be a sort of "decompression stop" for you if you are attempting to ascend from a deep loss and that my words might speak to your pain in a way that would offer you comfort and hope as you slowly ascend.

Thoughtful Theology

"Where can I go from Your Spirit?
Where can I flee from Your presence?
If I go up to the heavens, You are there.
If I make my bed in the depths, You are there."

- Psalm 139:7-8

<u>christmas key.</u>

Isn't it strange God chose to come
not as a warrior but a child,
to endure man's "good intentions"
so disloyally defiled?

No deeds of our own goodness are good enough
that any man can brag,
falling far short of God's glory -
our righteousness to Him is but a rag.

Only One provision could ever be
unblemished in God's sight,
that's why God sent His Babe of innocence
to set us free from this world's plight.

Though God Himself, He suffered much
a life victorious over pain,
so when we'd too despair in trials
His mighty strength through us would reign.

Our God, how He must love us
to have paid the wages for our sins,
making His Son, our Righteous Bridge
joining His grace to sinful men.

Jesus Christ, the Lamb of God
a ransom for our debt that we might live,
to trust by faith upon His Name
His redeeming sacrifice did give.

Nailed to a cross at Calvary
He agonized our dreaded fate,
but do we recognize our Savior
in the deadness of our state?

Goodwill toward men and colored bows
buy not salvation's security,
no earthly gifts fit locks in heaven,
but Jesus Christ, our Christmas Key!

<u>do and do.</u>

Why has your soul become so downcast?
When in the race did you lose peace?
Where down the path did your foot stumble?
When did your runner's delight cease?

Have you made a covenant with death
through an agreement with the grave,
to "do and do" with "rule on rule"
chaining your spirit like a slave?

Have you forfeited grace's freedom
for legalism's yoke of slavery,
to be now burdened by your bondage
without a life of victory?

Are you held captive by some error,
flogged by a false philosophy,
depending on traditions of this world
rather than on Christ Who set you free?

Have you been thrown into confusion
by a perverted gospel preached,
which really is no gospel truth at all
if to win men's praises is beseeched?

Why as though you could become more righteous
are you trying to be justified by law,
when God credits His righteousness apart from works,
when from His grace did you withdraw?

Your righteousness is not contingent
on what for God your best has done,
but on what by grace He's done for you,
received as a free gift through His Son.

If righteousness could be gained through law,
Christ's crucifixion was in vain;
No one is justified by law,
blamelessness before God can none obtain.

Rather, the law was put in charge to lead us
to our hope of glory - Christ within,
purposefully silencing each mouth
to make us conscious of our sin.

Christ is the final end of law.
His perfect life lived did fulfill
righteous requirements for sinful man
through Him accomplishing God's will.

The Lamb of God who knew no sin,
became world's sin on our behalf,
so He could cloth us in His righteousness
handing to us His power's staff.

He took the stinger out of sin,
offender's guilty judgment's nail,
through innocent hands to remove
the curse of law's dividing veil.

So if your underneath the law
you give sin's power a foothold,
but Christ became a curse for all!
Death's victory has been annulled!

His ransom paid the debt for many
once and for all and not again,
now lawless acts have been forgiven
leaving no sacrifice for sin.

Now those in Christ are not condemned
because through Christ new order came,
setting aside "old" covenant for "new"
establishing the second to remain.

Christ's death has qualified you
His co-heir, entitled saint,
through a new will put in effect
by holy blood no sin could taint!

<u>same grace.</u>

Sit down, O my weary soul
in the glory of God's grace,
at the right hand of the Great I Am
in throne room's Holy secret place.

For in Him dwelleth all the fullness
of the Godhead bodily,
and in Him you are complete
accepted in Christ righteously.

Strive then to enter Sabbath's rest
Creator's finished work made known,
abiding in God's love to bear good fruit
resting from toilsome work your own.

For if you're arduously spinning
in your own self-sufficiency,
are you not then but a potsherd
quarreling with your Creator's efficiency?

Shall the clay say to Him that fashions it,
"What makest Thou?" doubtful with demands.
Does your work admit mistrust
implying that the Potter has no hands?

Your worth is not based on what you do
but depends on Whose you are,
for you, His bride, did Christ once die,
how much more now, His shining star!

What greater value could your life have
than the purchase price for you Christ paid?
This is the measure of God's love for you -
how your significance is weighed.

The only thing that God says counts
is faith expressed through love,
for whatever is not from faith is sin
according to God's judgment from above.

So give up trying and start trusting
surrendering self-effort to the Lord.
Trust God's faithfulness to yield
your steadfast servant's full reward.

It's not by might, nor by your power
but by His Spirit, saith the Lord!
Labor not then in man's energy
no human resource can afford.

Abandon cursed commitments
determined to succeed, yet sure to fail,
get off your pride's performance treadmill -
let Spirit's wind spread out your sail.

Continue living by the same grace
just as at first your heart received,
being rooted and built up in Him
saved by your faith when you believed.

Be still, and know thy God.
Find rest in Him alone,
knowing the mystery - Christ within you
living raised Life through you, His own.

<u>no fear in love.</u>

There is no fear in love,
for perfect love drives out all fear,
because fear has to do with punishment
so dispel lies when dread is near.

Christ took our deserved scourging
and paid sin's unpaid penalty,
now by His strips we have been healed
to serve Him by grace thankfully.

So don't allow wages of sin
to lock your spirit up in fear.
Silence with truth your mind's Accuser
taking captive his threats you hear.

Take by faith God at His Word
trusting His ways are not your ways.
Stand on His truth as your foundation
when swells of doubt begin to sway.

Setting your mind on things above,
renew God's truth within your mind.
Walking by faith and not your feelings,
sift out all erring thoughts that bind.

Fill your fears as heavenly wells
with love's out pouring sacredness,
quieting your soul to Christ's reflection
when ring's ripple unsettledness.

Cast away your anxious cares
upon He Who gives His guarantee,
that Thou wilt keep in perfect peace
whose mind is stayed on Thee.

<u>drink of life.</u>

Take no thought about tomorrow
what you shall drink or you shall eat,
but seek ye first His kingdom
presenting God your needs to meet.

Humble yourself under God's mighty hand
that He may lift you up in His due time,
remaining prayerful in your circumstance
thankful to Him in the meantime.

Grieve not God's Holy Spirit
murmuring self-centered wining woe,
but with your heart sing psalms and praises
acquiescing to God's joyous overflow.

Then like a well-spring never failing,
His flowing fount will quench your needs,
seeping deep through sun-scorched fissures
to drench cracked ground's embedded seeds.

Come then all you who are thirsty
to drink of Life that satisfies,
to be refreshed - a thriving garden
perfumed with blooms to testify.

<u>game changer.</u>

Rage into riches,
message from mess,
beauty from ashes,
more out of less.

My Blessed Redeemer
Who turns scars into stars.
The Key Who unlocked
my imprisoning bars.

Rebuilder of ruins,
Restorer of streets,
Victory for losses,
Your death for defeats.

Your plus sign for minuses,
took the sting out of sin,
Your bridge crossed my far hearts
wide chasm within.

Living Water replaced
my servant girl's waterpot,
with Your internal well
my freedom You bought.

El Shaddai — all-sufficient —
my soul's nourishing breast.
I'm a spring of Your sweetness
Your fountain has blessed.

Songs for my shame,
Your mercy exchanged.
My pot's shattered pieces
Your wheel rearranged.

Value from vengeance,
purpose from pain,
meaning from madness
my loses for gain.

When in my backsliding state
I'd gone from bad into worse,
Your strong saving Hand
put my curse in reverse.

From my pit to Your palace,
You captured my queen out of danger,
Mighty Sovereign Chess Master,
My only God, The Game Changer!

<u>**you are my body.**</u>

I love you, my lamb
beside streams flowing still,
resting in pastures of peace
lead into paths of His will.

I love you, my land,
watered for fruit to remain,
as you respond by receiving
grace's showering rain.

You are my altar of incense,
Thy Lord's sacred bowl,
for my fragrant praise offering's
surrendered soul.

How delightful you are
when words pour from your lips,
blending a mixture of gladness
for sweet wine His mouth sips.

What a pleasure you are
yielded vessel of mercy,
when waging your war
against sin's controversy.

Well done with wisdom,
my small City of Palms,
when your judges rule justly
and your courts render psalms.

I love you, tame mare,
letting His thighs master you,
ridden by your Righteous Rider
named Faithful and True.

How you run when controlled
by the reigns of His love,
harnessed and held close by heaven's
bridle from above.

What a medley of music
your living lyre plays,
for my mind's metered mode
to think God's higher ways.

Your harp's harmony hums
bridal hymns to my soul,
keeping my wedding march true
to my love anthem's goal.

In you I rejoice, my cracked jar,
earthly clay marred with sin,
when you submit your flesh
to God's power within.

For you are my body,
God's temple of prayer,
whose only known beauty
is God's glory you bare.

handcrafted heart.

God-designed, not a ditto.
Fearlessly made, not a fraud.
Ethereally etched, not an echo.
Uniquely framed, not facade.

Born an original,
not to die as a copy.
Distinctly gifted by God,
not culture's photocopy.

Created to create -
His work of art to make art.
Not a plagiarized piece,
but a handcrafted heart.

Authentic not synthetic,
not man's mimicry.
Wonderfully woven,
not feigned forgery.

A masterpiece of thy Maker,
made not to sit on a shelf,
but to shine forth the truth
of your shimmering self.

Not cast in man's shadow,
nor hid under a bowl
to be robbed of your radiance
another has stole.

Not to live as a knockoff,
a copped-out copycat
counterfeiting your style
wearing another man's hat.

Your Potter has purposed
your shape for His glory -
to express the true light of
Creator's love story.

Honor your Artist –
your structure's Architect
with a life where reality
and faith intersect.

<u>**passion's favorite prisoner.**</u>

Whose influence are you under?
What spirit has your mind's control?
What thief or robber have you threatened?
What precious treasure has he stole?

Have you surveyed your soul lately?
Done an inventory of your life?
What's causing quarreling inside you?
What is the reason for your strife?

Have you found fulfillment within
or is your deep abyss depressed?
Where is your hunger's satisfaction?
Where is you inner being's rest?

Give thought now to your ways!
You drink, but never have your fill.
You eat, but never have enough.
You put on clothes, and are cold still.

All the counsel you've received
has only proved to wear you out.
Have your psychologists yet saved you
having heard your desperation's shout?

Yet you consult among the dead
on behalf of one who seeks to live,
when only one Man holds the key
and only He has life to give?

What have you gained from your hard labor?
Are you at the end yet of your rope?
Isn't now the time to reconsider
a new way of life and living hope?

You've watched your drug become your master,
slave driven by your source of sorcery.
Aren't you your passion's favorite prisoner
chained by your will's captivity?

You've 12-stepped to many meetings,
but are your soul's cravings constrained?
Have you yet found a higher power
that keeps your restless flesh restrained?

<u>think about your thinking.</u>

Think about your thinking.
Take thought about your thoughts.
Assess your mental process –
what lies you may have bought.

Do a check-up from your neck up.
Cross-examine your cognition.
Is your mind's engine running clean?
Or is there trash in your transmission?

Expose enshrouded error.
Dispel darkness' deceit.
Uproot untilled untruths.
Uncover camouflaged conceit.

Put on trial worldly wisdom.
Test out false philosophy.
Examine theories and opinions.
Scrutinize vain sophistry.

Do a check-up from your neck up
casting down imaginations
and every high and lofty thing
formed from exalted speculations.

Like a wise discerning DJ
choose well a faith-filled frequency
listening to a broadcast based on Truth
dialed into Divine decency.

Think about things lovely.
Think about things true.
Think about things noble,
not of things that make you blue.

Set your mind on things above,
not on fears that are below
where waves of worries billow
tossing feelings to and fro.

A double minded man
is unstable in his ways.
So fix your eyes on Jesus.
Call not to mind your former ways.

Let go of what's behind.
Pressing on towards what's ahead.
Lay hold of your inheritance
in what God's promises have said.

With your gaze set straight before you,
be not mindful from where you came,
but seek ye first God's kingdom
keeping Heaven's hope your aim.

God will keep in perfect peace
the mind whose stayed on Thee.
Meditate upon God's Word
trusting His Truth will set you free!

Shulamite's swan song.

You know my husband Solomon.
He wrote the Song of Songs -
His skewed version of our "fairytale"
excluding all his wrongs.

He made our Cinderella story
sound like a marriage so ideal.
The only problem was his truth was
a fish-story quite unreal.

How very happy could I be?
How truly cherished could I feel?
When such important information
He did not share, but did conceal.

Sol owned 300 concubines
and he had 700 wives!
That puts a new spin on our "fairytale"
and tells the real truth of our lives!

So the next time you're at a wedding,
listening to Sol's version running long,
just remember all his lovers
and my true Shulamite's swan song!

<u>**ways of the wind.**</u>

Immortal, not I
Mediator, not me
Savior, not self
Holy, only is He.

Yet while a sinner,
my payment He paid,
Forgiven forever
because Christ obeyed.

A ransom to reconcile
God's Lamb for the lame
Provision provided -
His blood for my blame.

God's Son for my sins
His death for my debt,
The cross for the curse,
His triumph for threat.

Resurrected Rainbow!
my Redeemer was raised
the Life-Giver lifted -
let thy Promise be praised!

Free gift, not my getting,
my choice now to choose
if my soul shall be saved
or my life will I lose.

Belief, not behavior
Heart, not just head
Decide, not deserve
Divine for the dead.

Confess, not to cover
Trust, and not try
Faith, not my flesh
Bow, not to buy.

Grace, not my goodness
Turn to Him, not by task
His mercy, not merit
Not achieve, but to ask.

Robe, not my rags
Crown, not corrupt
Splendor, not shamed
Bride, not bankrupt.

Christ, not a custom
Truth, not tradition
Reborn, not a ritual
Come, not cognition.

Gospel, not gods
Deliverer, not deeds
Man, not a method
Calvary, not creeds.

Relate, not religion
know Him, not just know of
Heaven, not hollow
not from below, but above.

New birth, not a nuance
Conversion, not my conduct
Regeneration, not rebuff
Condition, not to construct.

Inner man, not improve
Possess, not profess
Impart, not my image
Impute, not impress.

Love, not legalism
Liberty, not the Law
Life, not the letter
Woo, not withdraw.

Correct, not condemn
Light, not a lie,
Word, not this world
Renew, not retry

Transformed, not to toil
Fruit, not my fight
Wisdom, not warrior
Meek, not my might.

Sail, not to strive
Rest, not to row
Float, not to flail
not to force, but to flow.

Wings, not war horses
Ease, not expend,
Soar, not by sweat -
in the ways of the wind.

Lily, not labor
Flower, not fist
Bloom, not my battle
Immerse, not insist.

Boundaries, not bondage
Chaste, not in chains
His pleasure, not prisoner
Separate, not slain.

Borders, not binders
Cup, not to crave
Lot, not lie in wait
Shadow, not slave.

Loosened, not locked up
Released, not rebel
Justice, not jailhouse
Court, not a cell.

Measure, not madness
Scale, not be swayed
Portion, not poisoned
Proper, not plagued.

Fair, not in frenzy
Portion, not prowl
Weigh, not a wolf
Honest, not howl.

Strait, not seduced
Limit, not lust
Even, not excess
Upright, not unjust.

Useful, not usury
Level, not long
Equal, not exploit
Righteous, not wrong.

Bridled, not bribery
Harnessed, not hoard
Tamed, not temptation
Disciplined, not discord.

Reigned, not be ruled
Trained, not tyrannized
Controlled, not consumed
Power, not paralyzed.

Restraint, not to ravage
Resolved, not wrestling
Relaxed, not to rush
Resigned, not reveling.

Sword, not be swallowed
Defend, not devoured
Armored, not allured
Obey, not overpowered.

Wait, not in want
Patient, not proud
Content, not conceit
Listening, not loud.

Prepare, not poverty
Prevent, not pollute
Plan, not be pressured
Protect, not pursuit.

Stable, not staggering
Sober, not sick
Sound minded, not stumbling
Peace, not panic.

Harmony, not hostile
Simple, not stressed
Balanced, not busyness
Temperate, not test.

Worship, not worry
Behold, not bear
Willing, not working
Depend, not despair.

Tower, not terror
Stronghold, not scared
Fortress, not fearful
Shield, not be snared.

Dwelling, not dreading
Feathers, not fret
Refuge, not running
Temple, not threat.

Verdant, not violent
Greenery, not greed
Banquet, not beaten
Banner, not bleed.

Pasture, not plundered
Flock, not be fanged
Sheepfold, not slaughtered
Him, not harangued.

<u>loneliness.</u>

L once was my love,
   incomplete, unfulfilled

O once was me, the offender,
   God called pridefully willed

N once was my nothingness
   crying deep down inside

E once was my ear,
   though had heard still denied

L when I listened
   while Christ knocked at my door

I was His invitation
   I chose to ignore

N once was Christ's Name,
   I'd rejected as Lord

E once was Eternity,
   I'd spend in hell's ward

S once was Satan, the deceiver
   who sold me his lie

   But my loneliness ended
   because now

S is my Savior
   Who for me came to die

D.O.A.

It's natural to be religious,
but supernatural to be reborn,
entering this world physically alive,
though D.O.A., spiritually stillborn.

Know what you sow will never live
unless at first the kernel dies,
It must be planted in the natural
so that the spiritual can rise.

The man who loves his life will lose it.
The man who hates it, his shall keep.
The one who sows to please the Spirit
eternal life will his soul reap.

For flesh gives birth to flesh,
therefore, you must be born again.
Only the Spirit can birth spirit -
It is God's wind phenomenon.

Relational Rhythms

"The engulfing waters threatened me.
The deep surrounded me.
Seaweed was wrapped around my head.
To the roots of the mountains I sank down.
The earth beneath barred me in forever.
But You, Lord my God,
brought my life up from the pit."

- Jonah 2:5-6

<u>**a mute heart's scream.**</u>

How could they know
my pain so deep,
these agonizing tears
I weep?

Unheard am I,
a mute heart's scream
an inner madness
does it seem?

A shrieking torture
slays my soul,
my aching echo
takes control.

No peace indwells
my sparring space,
but fear instead
invades that place.

My mind attempts
to ear explain,
its hearing of
my dragging chain.

What kind of God
calls straight life truth,
knowing this way
I've warred since youth?

A God who calls
my love deceit;
"self-indulgent,"
"vain conceit."

"Idolater"
"inflamed with lust,"
Is this Thy Word
my heart should trust?

A God that calls
my love a lie,
"exchanging truth."
Guilty, am I?

Worshipping God's
created things?
Shall this be worth
what judgment brings?

Shall I forfeit my soul
for her embrace,
never to see
my Maker's face?

My choice to choose
of death or life.
Will hell consume
my endless strife?

Or shall I forsake
all I am,
for life offered through
God's sinless lamb?

Shall I give up
what I cannot keep,
for heaven's riches
that I'd reap?

To gain rewards
I could not lose,
obeying ways
my choice would choose.

Shall I lose my life
that I should find
God's healing
for these eyes so blind?

To know a hope
in days to come,
that through God's grace
I'd overcome…

My heart's desire
to gratify
my sinful nature's
raging cry.

For a new heart
would my Lord give me!
A new creation
would I surely be!

Not left in my own strength
to change,
but empowered
by God's gift exchange.

To grow in grace
where love abounds
and victory of
the Cross resounds.

His finished work!
No more for me,
but walk beside Him
humbly.

Forgiven sin!
the canceled code
nailed to the tree -
lawbreakers load!

No condemnation
to accuse,
No sting of sin
for death to use.

No more required
sacrifice.
Once and for all
He paid the price!

Made righteous
though no part my own,
but Christ's
my blamelessness is known.

Out of the tomb
no stone could keep,
His power to wake
my soul from sleep.

Arisen Savior!
from dark came light,
to call me out
from dungeon's night.

For freedom
Christ has set me free,
to be not bound
by slavery.

Though flesh may fail
His greater grace,
imparting Promise
to replace.

Raised up with Him
seated, I rest,
in Him, His peace,
I now possess.

<u>t'was once my rose.</u>

T'was once my rose,
though now my thorn,
she is,
since now I am reborn.

She laid by me,
though since did leave,
because to Him
we both must cleave.

Hers only
did my heart belong,
now beating weak
to be made strong.

That Christ's strength alone
may rest on me,
to be my soul's
sufficiency.

For His Name sake,
single I'll be,
trusting His grace
sustaineth me.

Though not without
true love fulfilled,
For He has come
and I am healed.

No other lover
set me free,
but Him alone
alive in me.

So now I choose
His will not mine,
my own desires
to resign.

For my Maker
is my Husband now,
my Only God,
to Whom I'll bow.

<u>**your Judas kiss.**</u>

Best friends betrayal,
your Judas kiss.
My dignity
you did dismiss.

Your spider's words
webbed to deceive,
in faith, I trusted
and believed.

O, but, what a
fool was I,
that I did buy
black widow's lie.

Falling for
false truths you told,
your word of honor -
just fools gold!

Swearing to
your own heart's hurt,
but then, your oath
you did desert.

Your broken promise
I hold now,
and in my cup
your empty vow.

But God's my Portion!
He redeemed
my dignity
that you demeaned!

Your pillaged pledge
that brought disgrace
He traded in for
saving grace!

He took the rags
you wrapped me in
and cloaked me in
His garment's grin.

His robe of righteousness
declared -
I'm free from bars
your shame had snared.

The evil that you
meant for harm,
God changed to good
with His strong arm.

My God He worked
all things for good
when by His side,
alone I stood!

<u>**bless not curse.**</u>

When first strike stung
my tender cheek,
my fierce flesh forced
my spirit weak.

My seething soul
sought to repay,
my enemy
for her display.

So schemed did I
of how I might
avenge my wronged
entitled right.

For surely judgment
must prevail.
Deserved justice
must not fail.

But then God's Spirit
spoke to me
the words He cried
at Calvary.

"Forgive them for
the things they do,"
so how can vengeance
I pursue?

While yet still sinners
Christ did die,
as mockers mocked
His death nearby.

So as His child
then who am I
to render my own
wrath's reply.

But then beyond
forgiveness paid,
He offered grace
on scales unweighed.

Life's gracious gift,
no riches spared,
to all, His love
remains declared!

To bless not curse
to this I'm called,
but how can I
when so appalled?

As anger burns
my fields with rage,
how can my revenge
not engage?

"No mercy!" screams
my heart's desire,
consumed by my
offended fire.

But grace must reign
my temper's course,
God's Spirit
I must not divorce.

For only love
from Him can flow,
if I'm to bless
my faulted foe.

So help me God
to die to self,
and put my pride
upon Your shelf.

That she might grasp
Your grace inside,
my fleshly frame
undignified.

Then holding love
she'd walk away,
blessed by my
hot-baked jar of clay.

forbidden love.

In front, she drives,
I trail behind,
we travel separate,
the road to wind.

She brakes too slow,
tail lights flash red,
now close, I see
her eyes ahead.

Framed in a mirror,
she looks at me,
reflecting back
our tragedy.

Her soul reveals,
the trial we share,
forbidden love,
so wrong, but rare.

I meet her gaze
through tears I cry,
and send her back
my heart's reply.

I see your exit's
coming near,
go on your way
and do not fear.

I wave good-bye
and blow a kiss,
to let her know
her love I'll miss.

Go far, my sweet,
away from me,
for grace and truth
to set you free.

<u>**cross' kiss.**</u>

Of love...
we often say, "I feel,"
"infatuation,"
"strong appeal."

Responding to
emotions voice,
we let impulses
make our choice.

Though higher love
did God display,
to show us
a far greater way.

Greater love
has no one than this,
that One should die
for Calvary's kiss.

To demonstrate
how love should give,
so we could see
how we should live.

A life of daily
sacrifice,
forever long
not once or twice.

Yielding our will
for other's best,
surrendering
our prideful quest.

To love in truth
and also deed,
not letting mere words
supersede.

Forgiving as
the Lord forgave,
because my soul
His life did save.

So let our love
be known by this -
our self-denying
Cross' kiss.

<u>withdraw.</u>

I had a friend
I called Withdraw,
whose eyes denied
the tears they saw.

Who seeking shelter
built walls in vain,
to keep her safe
from deeper pain.

Within her fence
she sealed her soul,
crouching her truth
in fear's foxhole.

I wish I could have
crossed her moat,
when her heart's cry
seemed so remote.

Her tucked tendrils
were soft to touch,
but seldom ever
opened much.

Afraid a stroke
might break her stem,
she closed her bloom's
sweet fragrant gem.

I wish I'd held
the calloused claw,
of my furled friend
I called Withdraw.

Agony's Archive

"From inside the fish Jonah prayed to the Lord his God.
He said: "In my distress I called to the Lord,
and He answered me.
From deep in the realm of the dead I called for help,
and You listened."

- Jonah 2:1

frozen nightmare.

Where's my summer? Where's my spring?
Where's the warmth sunshine would bring?

I'm caught by ice's wintery bite,
I'm lost inside it's dead of night.

A season stuck where snowflakes cling
with blizzard's wicked windy sting.

No seasons come. No seasons go.
No mountain highs, just valley's low.

A season stuck where seeds don't bloom.
Where darkness grips with gloves of doom.

Where winter whips wounds that won't mend -
My gauntlet's run that has no end.

A time to mourn, a time to weep,
when will my gladness get to reap?

When will I have my victory dance?
When will my laughter have a chance?

A season stuck in suffering,
where torment has no buffering.

Where did my change of season hide?
When did God's grace and hell collide?

When will my heavy heart not grieve?
Where is the Hope I can believe?

When will my shattered soul find peace?
When will my frozen nightmare cease?

<u>**gift of good-byes.**</u>

The tears I cry lately
fall fast from my face
with no hope of comfort
- no sign of God's grace.

The tears I cry lately
flow streams of red blood
through shattered soul windows
- a wounded heart's flood.

No good end to wait for.
No season to cease.
No rest for the weary.
No promise of peace.

Just pain when i rise.
Just pain when sun sets.
Just pain for existence
that never forgets.

The tears I cry lately
I'll sow, so I'll reap -
sadness for gladness
divine riches I'll keep.

Affliction for access,
difficulty for doorway,
oppression for opening,
gallows for gateway.

Grief into glory,
healing from hurt,
disgrace into dignity,
harvest from dirt.

Pools out of pits,
springs from sinkholes,
drinks from depression,
blessings from bowls.

The tears I cry lately
have dried from my eyes
having learned to embrace
my gift of good-byes.

<u>**lose and choose.**</u>

The Lord giveth.
The Lord taketh away.
"Blessed be the Lord,"
I'll say.

Another loss
I've learned to grieve
because to Him
my soul must cleave.

Another thing
that I have lost,
but God is good
despite my cost.

Another friend
has shown betrayal,
but God's sure love
shall never fail.

Another arrow
pierced a leak,
but in Christ, I'm strong
although I'm weak.

Another illness
wars within,
but by His stripes
He took my sin.

I've learned from loss.
I've learned to lose
since by my faith
His grace I choose.

The Lord giveth.
The Lord taketh away.
"Blessed be the Lord,"
I'll say.

<u>you called me beloved.</u>

You called me beloved
and reeled my heart in.
All Your soft wooing words
got deep under my skin.

You got what You wanted
my heart, mind, and soul.
My whole being's breath
Your mere presence had stole.

My hedge You then lifted
for my soul to lay bare
to endure the cruel stripes
of Your scourging nightmare.

I asked for some bread
and You kicked me a stone
from the foot of Your glorious
high lofty throne.

Where is my Lost Lover?
Where did He go?
Where is Your embrace
my soul used to know?

Why did You kiss me
so gently at night
just to render me weak
so my lips You could smite?

Your eyes I once trusted
to cure with concern
have become suns of fire
inciting my burn.

The Hands that caressed
Your small trusting dove,
now strike her teared cheek
in a form You call love.

What is love Mr. Lover?
By Your Word it is kind,
Yet benevolence hides
and Your grace I can't find.

Where is Your safe tower
my soul-keeping King?
Where is the soft comfort
of Your love's feathered wing?

In my shadow of death,
I strain looking for light
while my faith and experience
battle and fight.

Should I take off my Beloved's
gold promising ring
still echoing tales
of the love He would bring?

Where is my Good Shepherd
Who comforts His lamb?
Why did He retreat
without giving a damn?

The Lord is my slayer.
In thorned pastures I lie.
My spirits laid wanting
and waiting to die.

Beside poisoned waters
I followed Your lead.
From Your Shepherd's clenched fist
I sat waiting to feed.

Oh Bountiful One -
once my Great El Shaddai,
You said that You'd come
when You heard my heart cry.

But without a good-bye
my love You forsook.
My heart, mind, and soul
were the plunder You took.

You buried my hope
in a shallow mass grave.
My trust and endearment
You chose not to save.

<u>**comfort me my christian friend.**</u>

Comfort me, my Christian friend,
heal me with your words.
Tell me how God guards his flock
and always feeds His birds.

You ask me with a smile
if I've wanted to get well.
Where is your faith, you sickling?
- while you bid me a farewell.

My body's illness slays me,
but your words hurt even more.
You blame me for my sickness
thinking my heart you did restore.

"Things happen for a reason,"
you say tritely when I'm down.
Why not throw me out an anchor
so a drowning man can drown.

"God will never give you
any more than you can bear,"
then you tack on that you love me
and you're holding me in prayer.

"No burden is too heavy."
"A bruised reed He will not break."
"Be not weary in well-doing."
"Your bleeding heart He won't forsake."

Oh, thank you, Christian friend
for all the comfort you bestow,
but my bruised reed has been broken
and my valley is too low.

My burden is too heavy
for your "Footprints" poem to sustain.
My despair is too dark
to bear the bright bliss that you feign.

So please save your sinking Scriptures
and Romans 8 verse 28.
Spare my heartbreak from your comfort
and let the Bible's sweet psalms wait.

<u>**my case against your goodness.**</u>

You claim to be a good God,
compassionate and kind,
yet, neglect for helpless souls
is all my saddened eyes can find.

You said Your glorious riches
would surely meet my needs,
and yet, You turn a deaf ear
to my bleeding heart that pleads.

A fortress for protection?
A shadow to abide?
Yet, nowhere can I run to.
I've got no place left to hide.

You clothe Your precious lilies
in divine splendor, they are dressed,
yet, naked, I kneel praying
amidst green grasses You have blessed.

Am I to feel as valued
as Your splendor's petaled stars
when the only thing I have to wear
are open wounds and scars?

You feed Your little sparrows,
wine and dine Your darling doves.
You're a good God Who cares deeply
for the lives and things He loves.

It must be I'm to blame then
for my hunger and my want
slowly starving in this pasture
You've watched idly become my haunt.

My harp is tuned to mourning.
My flute can only wail.
No words of mine are justified
to speak of Your betrayal.

There are no angels in my corner.
No Christian court will lend an ear
to hear my case against Your goodness -
Your reputation's free and clear!

How greedy and ungracious of me
to think to ask for more
when granting me safe food and clothes
You see as such a chore.

Shame on me of "little faith"
for seeing truth playout as lies.
"For blessed am I who mourns and grieves,"
- my broken spirit cries.

How sick am I who suffers
with a heart that spurns Your praise?
Where is Your faithful servant –
Your grateful child that obeys?

Please forgive me, Oh Good God
now that I find You hard to trust,
after my prayers have gone unheard so long
that my tears have turned to rust.

how i wonder where you are.

Baby Jesus, Superstar,
How I wonder where You are?

Twelve long years, with no prayers heard.
I've begged for mercy – and still no word.

You mock my moans. You watch me wail.
You laugh as my torn feathers flail.

My broken wings, You trample on.
My bleeding heart, You spit upon.

You chuckle at my feeble crawl.
You kick me curled up in a ball.

Your Holy Hand, You'll not extend,
too high, too right, for love to lend.

You see me shaking on the street,
few clothes to wear with sandaled feet.

Yet, no warmth would You offer me
No plea of mine would You agree.

To my tears, Your angels sing,
"Glory to the newborn King!"

Red and green lights blink and glow,
Your Heaven's help has yet to show.

<u>**have mercy on me Jesus.**</u>

Oh Lord, won't you put me
outa' my misery?
My body's racked with torture
and clothed with agony.

Please find an 18-wheeler
a speedin' down a hill.
Don't let it stop 'til heaven
with my grin on its grill.

All hopes been forgotten.
My air is despair.
Have mercy on me Jesus
and show me that You care!

Lord, push me from a tower
and splat me on a road.
Fix me up like road kill
- A death a la mode!

Send a mean hillbilly
a loadin' up his gun.
Make sure he's got a clean shot.
Let's get this damn job done!

Have mercy on me Jesus
and get me outa' here.
Use any means available
cuz I ain't got no fear!

A white shark would thrill me.
A grizzly bear would do.
Just serve me up for supper
and let me be their stew!

Hang me from a tall tree
and lynch me with a rope.
A long syringe would be fine
filled with lethal dope.

Lord, prove that You love me
and take me away.
Strike me down with lightning.
Don't wait another day.

Cuz I can't bear this suffering.
I've got way too much pain.
Oh Lord, take me home -
for to die is to gain!

<u>**caretaker of Job.**</u>

Why is life given
to those in despair,
and breath to a soul
left to writhe in its snare?

What loving Father
lets groans go unheard
so hearts become sick
after hope's been deferred?

If misery was measured
and suffering had scales,
no mountain would outweigh
my heart's wounded wails.

Where is my Good Shepherd
Who guardeth His flock?
Where is my Protector?
My foundation's Sure Rock?

Caretaker of Job -
am I now Your new prey
so Your glory and grandeur
my pain can display?

Are You not big enough
just to leave me alone?
Must You torture my frailty
deep down to the bone?

Have I become Your target
to punish and pierce
with Your sharp angry arrows
so stabbing and fierce?

How can I love such a God
Who has lowered His hedge?
Where is Your safe shield
Your truth's Word did allege?

Ashes to ashes,
dust back to dust.
Yet though He slay me,
in Him will I trust.

<u>**eyes of dying.**</u>

I look into
these eyes of dying
helpless heartache
ever crying.

Dead dreams gaze
from graves of hope
these eyes of dying
trying to cope.

Staring back
from misery
a mirror mourns
in front of me.

These eyes of dying
bear a soul -
a smothered flame
long-suffering stole.

Prophetic Parables

"Out of the depths I cry to You, Lord.
Lord, hear my voice.
Let Your ears be attentive
to my cry of mercy.
If You, Lord, kept a record of sins,
Lord, who could stand?
But, with You there is forgiveness."

- Psalm 130:1-4

<u>I Am, I Am.</u>

I heard a pounding knock outside
my heart home's chained closed door,
and looking through the peephole
there I saw, a god I'd seen before.

"Please take my money," said I-Have,
better known by his good friends as Possession.
"Won't you work for me and worship me
so I can consume you with obsession?"

I replied, "Your currency is counterfeit.
It's not the means I need to live.
What would it profit me to gain the world,
enslaving my soul as your captive?"

Then up stepped Works of Righteousness,
"Practice my religious vain traditions.
Accept my package wrapped in piety
and my pride's meriting additions."

I replied,
"Your righteousness is all man-made,
based on good deeds you think you do,
I need a righteousness from God,
I won't unlock my door for you."

Following Works, came Self, his righteous brother,
"I'm the other performing twin, I-Do.
Seek my self-grandeur and vainglory
to give your worth its false value."

I replied, "Vanity can't fill me.
I am a heart that longs for love.
My dark and empty living room
misses its live-in from above."

"Nonsense!" screamed the god, I-Feel,
"I'll fill your empty heart so high,
with the intoxicating sparkle
of my red wine's seductive lie."

I said, "Your god's emotions are unstable
like wild waves tossed to and fro,
I need an unwavering peace.
I think your wine I will forego."

He said,
"Come then, meet my sister.
I know you'll like Experience.
She speaks in tongues while clashing cymbals
to get your home an audience."

I said,
"Displaying signs and miracles
are not substantial evidence,
to prove a spirit comes from God
despite her god's self-confidence.

Even Satan masquerades
as a white angel dressed in light.
I'll not respond to the deception
of her well-disguised invite."

Then I-Think came up strutting,
"I am so wise in my own eyes.
Follow only logic that you understand,
allowing no god to lord, but I!"

I said, "I see your beliefs are sincere,
unfortunately, sincerely wrong
because the just shall walk by faith.
Depart! Your god is too headstrong."

He replied,
"Here comes my cousin, Relative
who thinks God's sun has many rays.
He rejects God's truth as absolute
so he can follow his own ways."

Relative said,
"I know God says Christ is the Way
but my path to God is through another.
I will not take the Bible literally
or in its light my sin would smother.

God and I have a relationship.
It's just with me he knows his place.
He understands my spirituality is different
that our terms just don't interface."

I said,
"But how can two walk close together
except they be agreed?
God will not change His way of truth
to match the error of your creed.

You're headed down into death's chamber
like a lost sheep off to be slain.
I will not open for your follies call
fooled by your waywardness of Cain."

"Wait!" cried out I-Try with purpose,
"My good intentions give life meaning.
Rely on human efforts for your credit,
so on your strength you will be leaning."

I said, "I am too tired to depend on
my own willpower's failing might.
I need strength supernaturally
to help me win my soul's lost fight."

"Not Thy will, but mine be done!"
I-Will asserted with superiority.
"Continue with my plans. I'm Independence,
unyielded to divine authority!"

I said, "The True God stands opposed to pride.
But to the humble, He gives grace.
Be off! You're not the god I'm looking for.
Turn back your rebel's mocking face."

Then a gentle knock tapped on my heart.
"Who's out there calling on my name?
What do you have to buy that satisfies?
What is the reason that you came?"

"My name is Jesus. I am I AM.
I stand before your broken heart
not as a false god or a salesman,
but to give you life and a new start."

I said, "Oh really, Mr.....was it.....I AM?
I'm sure your new beginning has a price.
Not to mention what I've always heard
redemptions based on being nice.

But go ahead and leave me with the bill I owe
and slip your life-product under my door
so I can keep my hard heart's chain on
taking just Your gift while You ignore."

I AM responded,
"My precious present is a free gift.
It can't be purchased at your cost.
Neither by one's riches nor one's goodness
can a soul be bought when it is lost.

The purchase price that God requires
is by grace through faith alone
that you believe in Me and then receive
the resurrected life I own.

I came and laid down My own life for yours
so my atoning trust could be your tender
that if you'd see your need then ask to borrow,
I could be your overdrawn soul's value lender.

I'm not a religion for your front porch
to impress your neighbors that walk by.
I am your run-down heart's rebuilder.
Your sure foundation from on high!

I became flesh and dwelt among you
fulfilling God's law by what I've done
to impute My righteousness to you
giving you the victory that I've won.

I Am the Way, the Truth, and the Life!
No one comes to the Father but through Me.
I've come to fill your vacant heart
and set your chained up spirit free!"

Sliding off my chain of unbelief,
I opened up my closed heart, once alone,
and asked Jesus, "How much do you love me
though unworthiness is all I own?"

Stepping inside to make me whole,
His hands from heaven hugged my heart,
and I embraced my long lost love
as I AM's Spirit did impart.

<u>**maiden mission.**</u>

I entered in the fairy tales
once upon a night...
Would I find my waif in shredded rags
or cloaked in lily-white?

Is she the duckling among swans
or off kissing croaking frogs?
Would she click her heels three times
then vanish in a fog?

I traipsed through emerald forests.
Searched the candied house upon the hill.
I pushed Jack down and broke his crown
to make a play for Jill.

I climbed up broken beanstalks,
tossed my coins in wishing wells.
I listened for her faint-lit voice
in washed-up ocean shells.

Many a tall tower did I scale
trusting in Rapunzel's locks of hair,
hoping one day inside a window
I'd see my princess standing there.

I even spoke with Little Red Riding Hood
just the other day.
She said she saw her sitting
in some underground cafe'.

"Now how am I gonna find her
when she's hangin' out with trolls
and here I'm forging castles
on some damsel damned patrol?"

But I never stopped believing
she was somewhere waiting to be free
though now imprisoned in the darkness
lost and left without a key.

Following my own yellow brick road,
I continued on the way right in my eyes
down to a sign at my path's end
locating my wayward soul's demise.

"Dead," it said. "Have I not life?
Did this sign speak truth of me?
Was I the damsel in the dungeon
locked up in death without a key?"

Beyond the sign, I saw a dwelling,
a cold gray mansion made of stone.
And though in fear, I ventured in
to explore its mystery unknown.

There I saw the mirror-mirror on the wall
framing me, no white knight on a horse,
but just a wicked witch reflecting back
black evil eyes full of remorse.

Right then, a light turned on inside me
exposing my illiterate dark heart
letting me read between the lines
so I could tell real-life apart.

"I've played the fool in my own tragedy
awaiting my life's final closing act
performing sin scripted by a Schemer
as his misled lady, Maniac!"

But far away from Auntie Em's house
having reaped whirlwind of wind I'd sown,
I had no Savior there to guide me
and be my lost soul's very own.

Then as I stared into the mirror,
behind my back appeared a Man
and with a gentle, caring Spirit
reached out to me His saving hand.

He said, "Alice lives in wonderland.
But if you'll turn and come to Me,
you'll surely find the missing princess
you yourself were made to be.

For out of a twisted wreath of thorns
I've made you your own majesty's jeweled crown
to bestow your head with grace and dignity
so your lost princess could be found."

I said, "Sorcerers with their wizardry
cursed my mind with deviled lies
deceiving me, I'd find fulfillment
if idolized through Cinderella's eyes.

But now I see no Snow White saves me
but that I'm made complete in You.
My maiden mission is mind fiction
I need not any more pursue.

It's truly I who slumber deeply
from green apples toxic bite
needing a Prince of Peace to kiss me
out of my princess' dead of night.

But now this mirror-mirror stands before me,
revealing my wretched witch's face.
Who can save my shrew from my sins?
Who will show my hexed hag grace?"

He said,
"I crossed sins off with My death sentence
breaking grave's binding cold embrace
and justified your offset margin
to reconcile you by My grace.

All your well-read and done transgressions
have been deleted from your page
through My new version's abridgment
I published once to pay your wage.

Now come to Truth and receive Life.
I am your Author and Perfecter.
I'll write your end a new beginning
and be your character's director."

I exclaimed,
"You're not folklore or a legend
or some anecdotal book's footnote.
You are the Christ saving Messiah
about Whom the Holy Spirit wrote!"

Thanking Emmanuel for mercy,
I bowed my heart down and confessed
repenting of my sin of unbelief
the mirror-mirror had addressed.

Turning around, I saw salvation
looking me deeply in the eyes.
Now face to face with my queen Maker.
I knew my tales He would revise.

He said,
"You're now My cherished princess,
having My royal family's Name
to be your righteousness and glory
void of indelibly inked blame!"

I said,
"My Prince of Peace has finally come!
His Word of life is my bestseller!
His Holy Spirit is my new release,
my heart imprint's Love Letter Dweller!"

<u>sandcastle queen.</u>

While building my sandcastle
with my queen at sea's shore,
You asked me to part
from the love I adored.

Not willing I'd splash
just my feet in Your tide,
You motioned me closer
ebbing Your voice alongside.

You said, "Remember that morning
coming by faith to My sea
when you confessed your sins
saying you believed in Me?

And how I washed you all clean
in My cool undertow,
regenerating your heart
with the grace of My flow.

All your sins I forgave.
My crosscurrent took them away,
drowning your sin debt forever
so you could live life a new way.

Now the life that you live
is Mine to be lived out through you,
so sinful passions you fight,
My Spirit's sea can subdue.

Though I see My shoal's shallows
are now your only appeal,
but the love that I offer
is deep, freeing, and real."

I said, "I've tried to change my lifestyle,
but I am what I am.
I've done nothing but fail
Your heterosexual exam?

I mean, it's not a bad habit
I'm attempting to quit.
You're asking me to be who I'm not
without a nature to fit.

Here on my beach, I'm accepted
a valued gay-Christian,
justifying my sin
as a genetic condition.

And here I've found teachers who preach
unsound doctrine by liars,
where in great numbers we gather
to suit and condone our desires.

So it's Your Word against mine,"
I cried out in defense,
"I'll define righteous conduct
based on my instinctive sense."

But without condemnation,
Your tender tide coaxed me in
to bath and refresh my
guilt conscience from sin.

You said,
"The righteousness that you own
was a gift to you from My sea,
making you right in My sight
to have a friendship with Me.

So come let your mind be renewed
by My truth's transforming spray
correcting your old way of thinking
that you were born to be gay.

Realize, I've changed your identity
you're now a brand new creation
reborn of My Spirit to fathom
the depth of My love's liberation.

You've been freed from the sandbars
that once jailed your desert heart's land
to enter My ocean's oasis
where your latitudes can expand."

I said, "I could never be happy
if I completely submit to Your will.
Can't I indulge my flesh
while pleasing You still?"

You said,
"My plan is to prosper, not harm you
to give you a future and hope,
but you'll forfeit My green grace
while there on your eroding slope.

You see the foundation you've built on
will be soon washed away,
but if you build upon Me,
your heavenly castle will stay."

Stuck and divided
between You and my world,
which one would I worship
would it be You or my girl?

I offered You everything else
but this idol I owned,
begging and pleading
You'd leave this sin alone.

But You said, "I love you, Beloved,
as no other will,
but I can't heal a heart
that insists to be ill."

Then I replied,
"Not by my might, nor my power
could I ever let go of the hand
that I've put on the throne
of my castle of sand."

You said, "Trust Me, I know well
your broken heart's pain
torn in half from inside
and of your head, half-insane.

But if you come unto to Me
and then by faith enter in,
I'll carry you out, liberated,
so our intimacy can begin.

Together we'll share an adventure.
I'll teach you to surf and to sail
if you'd just lay down your spade
and your heavy heart's rusty pail."

Then stepping in closer to You,
though still resisting Your way,
my heels sunk themselves deeper
held under by quicksand's delay.

I knew not then of the bondage
that had ensnared my feet,
until I tried to walk with You
from out of my bank of concrete.

But trusting Your ocean to float me
I knelt my knees down in Your foam,
asking for Your tide to take me
out into my new foreign home.

I prayed, "By faith, not my feelings,
I'm trusting Your Word to be true,
please help me to leave my known land
to enter Your vast freedoms blue.

And though still my mind's riddled
why my sexual preference offends,
I'll choose to yield to your currents
keeping my friends as just friends.

And if no other shall love me
as in the way I feel best,
Lord, be my comforting calm
so in Your peace, I will rest.

I'll seek Your lathering love
to keep my longings fulfilled
knowing Your grace is sufficient
for my wounded soul to be healed.

Please teach me to swim in Your channels
and how to float when I'm weak.
Help me to hear and obey
Your safeguarding swells when they speak.

Lord, let Your love be my strength
to accomplish this prayer that I pray,
that my life would bring glory
to Your Spirit's sea every day."

<u>**white dove's liberty.**</u>

Behind the blinds of my pane,
I heard a voice sweetly call,
"Show Me your face doubting dove,"
soft-sounding like gentle snowfall.

His voice spoke consoling my fears
from outside my tomb's stone-cold place,
saying, "Hear Me, come with Me
from out of your cave of disgrace."

Out of His lips poured compassion
more delightful than wine,
assuring me, "I am My lover's
and My lover is Mine."

Was this really my Lover?
But from here how could I know?
So wooed by His words
I sought my Divine Romeo.

Could it be me He was calling
His own love's doubting dove?
Can't He see I'm just but a pigeon,
feathered over my guilt-ridden glove?

Yet cautiously curious
I leaned toward the edge,
to substantiate claims
His promising words had alleged.

I heard Him say, "No fear can keep you
for through Me you are free,
from out of your cliff's prison cell
for I Am your white dove's liberty!

Why you are still living
as though spiritually dead,
when the grave did not keep Me
but I arose, as I'd said?

You need not be wearing
those old wings so torn,
over your new dove's bold wings
you received when you were reborn?

Have you not heard
or did you not know,
of the transformation you've had
and of your power also?"

I answered, "It's so dark in my cave,
of this dove, I could not see,
so I took back my old wings
from down off of the tree."

He said, "Because I know of your frailty
I gave you a spirit of power and love,
and exchanged your old wings for new
My free, though now, doubting dove.

Let Me explain what has happened
the moment you believed from My bird's-eye view,
upon trusting my word, not your wisdom
to be faithful and true.

Your perishing pigeon died long ago,
when through Adam entered sin,
leaving you dead in your trespasses
stuck in a flesh feathered coffin.

And God being perfectly holy
required an unblemished Lamb to suffice,
reconciling all to Himself
through One righteous Man's sacrifice.

That's why in your place I was crucified
that you too could be buried with Me,
So when I arose three days later,
in Me, you could find Life and be free.

So salvation is not just forgiveness
though My death fully balanced the Book,
paying your sin debt completely
- this spiritual justice it took.

But the gospel truth in its fullness
is a free gift to who in Me shall believe,
that though he were dead; yet shall he live
and in his heart, My Life receive.

But as long as you wear your self-effort
over My grace's new wings of love,
you'll be weighed down to heavy
to fly high like a dove.

Can you honestly tell Me
you've been truly set free?
Won't you come near the light,
maybe then you'll agree.

You never were meant
to stay in your old identity's tomb;
yet, your reality's become
this cave of a cocooning womb.

Just like the dark days of Noah,
when water flooded the earth,
He patiently stayed in the ark
then came out baptized in new birth.

So also to you I have brought
a freshly picked olive leaf
as a sign of your freedom
seeking your white dove's belief.

So reckon your past pigeon dead
for her twin has returned from on High,
with a new nature from heaven
to tell you the land's surface is dry.

If you'd remove your ark's cover,
you'd see the deep's founts have abated,
the mountain tops are exposed,
the sky's floodgates I've negated.

But like a rock garden locked up
or a spring shut closed and sealed,
is my doubting dove in her cleft
unwilling to trust Me and yield.

Won't you lay down your burden
and with Me come along,
for behold winter is past
the rain is over and gone!

My rainbow is a sign of My covenant
that I've rolled away your tomb's stone of reproach,
so now at My love's throne of grace
you can daily approach.

Your downcast dove's cry
has been heard through the land,
where your vineyard blooms wait,
do you now understand?"

I responded, "As though I was asleep,
yet my heart was awake,
I heard Your quiet voice knocking
asking for Your dove to take.

And I agree with Your truth,
I've never been truly set free,
having relied on myself
for my sufficiency."

Smiling, He said,
"I ask no performance from you
My wind sweeping grace won't enable,
but that you spread your new wings
upheld by My breeze to keep stable.

Then by your faith let Me lead you
as you look only to Me,
following the way through My eyes
only My Spirit can see."

So I prayed, "Awake, O north wind
and come wind of the south,
breath Your Spirit's sweet fragrance
as a new song for my mouth!"

Then stepping out into the day,
I, at once, regained my lost sight,
and set my mind to fly far away
from my dead pigeon's dark nest of night!

And while still feeling my fear,
I acted in faith anyway,
putting my hope in Him, ready
to be carried away.

Then with the little I knew of
this miraculous One undefiled,
I bounded out to find freedom
with the faith of an innocent child.

And that's how I entered this rest,
I have since come to know,
by trusting His Word, not my ways,
Christ's love's liberty did bestow.

Today soaring ever so freely
floating in peaceful blue bliss,
I'm so thankful His grace,
He did not let me miss!

<u>**scary to be a canary.**</u>

Sometimes it's scary to be a canary
where gases and smog fill the air
where chemicals fume and girls wear perfume
and ladies spray smells in their hair.

I'm just a small bird with my song gone unheard
that my body's felt sickened and ill
by solvents and paint that can poison and taint
silently leaking out gases that kill.

In the old days, coal miners would hear my chirps cry
finally heeding my songless bird's sign
but now, ears have been closed to my little bird's woes
and the doctors all tell me I'm fine.

Though my bright yellow feathers disguise my disease
and hide my condition from view,
my innards are burning and my stomach is churning
while some say my stories untrue.

This fire's unseen that consumes my bird's being
with flames raging out of control!
What we need is awareness about this unfairness
and to start a canary patrol.

My sensitive nature should sound the alarm
like it did for the miners of coal.
So please ponder my pain and the words that I'm saying
and make saving canaries our goal!

Dedicated to all those suffering from Multiple Chemical Sensitivities and Environmental Illness.

<u>captain of my soul.</u>

Wail, O ship, weep, O traitor
    left without harbor or home,
Woe to you, O destroyer,
    aimless seafarer, you roam.

You are the market of nations,
    multitude's merchandise,
doing business widespread,
    in all kinds of fine spice.

You satisfy distant districts
    and coastland customers,
thriving in much commerce
    to pay well your vain voyagers.

Bidding farewell saving straits
    you trusted your scurvy survey,
to bound blind in broad brine's
    self-willed wide-watered way.

Far-off lands are your lovers,
    many waters your men,
wandering 'bout in sea's wilds,
    you're playing the harlot again.

Woe to you, O loose winch,
    crosscurrent's unmoored concubine,
Woe to you, pleasure drifter,
    without any sight of shoreline.

Your awnings like eyelids
	flirt with purple and blues,
soliciting caulk from shipwrights
	for your weak seams to use.

Storing your innermost chambers
	with honey, oil, and grain,
you amass fortunes of balms,
	from high seas blue domain.

Loving the wage of your work,
	you exchange wood for your wares,
decking yourself with inlays
	of night's ebony fares.

You supply provinces passion,
	O you queen of kingdoms,
whoring your fisherman's hooker
	for unjust king's ransoms.

Sailors come alongside you
	intersecting your courtesan's path,
spreading wide-open your sails
	to refill your goblet with wrath.

A downdraft reeling drunkard,
	engulfed by mixed wine's swaying seas,
randomly ruddered, you stagger
	traversing crosswind's southerlies.

Woe to you, floating fugitive
	side-winding a wake running wild,
like a riotous rebel, you trail blaze your
	bloodshed defiled.

Like a loose tumbleweed,
	pursued by a sinking storm's gale,
as though chaff, you are tossed
	by winds sure to prevail.

All who handle your oars,
	and your oppressed galley slaves,
soon will go down with you sinking
	into depth's gangrene graves.

For the sea's scale has spoken
	having weighed your rig's revenue,
proclaiming your lost soul's shipwreck
	to your unconfessed crew.

Woe to you, shattered island
	now aground shoal's jagged-jaws,
laid to waste, widowed wreckage
	by truth's heavenly laws.

O broken-boned battleship,
	backlashed by blame on a beach,
salted snaps scourge your bilge,
	while breaker's bloody your breech.

Piercing peaks spear you,
      axing your unbraced boom down,
nailing your cold-cleated corpse
      inside your coffin to drown.

Now your whaler wounds wail
      caught by truth's harpooning sea,
Who can heal your hurt hull
      and set your broken bow free?

Rise up, O Captain of my soul,
      take first command of my small boat,
Rebuild and make my frail frame watertight,
      seaworthy by grace that I should float.

Rebuke and make rough rollers run,
      still surging seas down to a hush,
calm booming blues into a whisper
      tamed by Your strong arm's ruling rush.

Crush the head of my deep's serpent,
      churning up my mind's mire and mud,
straighten my crooked latitudes
      cursing my open grave throat's flood.

Bridle my reinless roaring waves
      whenever my white horses mount up,
Give me hope as my soul's anchor,
      to drink with steady hands salvation's cup.

Head me home towards heaven's harbor
        with my North's needle aiming true,
Turnabout my linen turncoats
        to seek the borders justice drew.

Set my sights upon Your lighthouse
        while through my tempest-gray to pass,
guide me with plumb line's centerboard
        through narrow gates of my impasse.

Clapping spinnakers applaud my jibe
        for I've cast about for a new sun,
to swallow up Your draft's decrees,
        plotting out my course already won.

I've thrown my heavy cargo overboard
        forsaking all riches of my own,
to serve and be Your faithful deckhand,
        with my soul's footstool at Your throne.

For to me, to live is Christ,
        dying to my old sea dog is gain,
No longer is my christened craft my own,
        but at my helm, Your hands shall reign!

Today, Your banner over me is love.
        Your navigator's Name do I extol.
You are on board, my Ancient Mariner!
        Thou art the Captain of my soul!

new moonflower.

My mind's eye wore world's sunglass
like a moon monocle framed haze,
that overcast my darkened heart
from Your bright being's beacon blaze.

When in the shadow of my blind spot,
eclipsed in dead of night I could not part;
You arose, My bloom's Day Breaker,
dawning first light inside my heart!

In Your voice, I heard green permanence
speak truth through Your light's lens,
clearing my clouded resolution
to see my mass You would transcend.

Descending to my soil's spoiled space,
You lowered divine vine's climbing ladder,
to raise me up from black hole's grave
out of my blighted bed's dead matter.

Lifting my faint face, low and faded,
towards Your Searchlight smiling from the sky,
You gazed, long-flamed at me, consuming me,
with grace's golden-rodded eye.

You sunkissed my death's dust cover,
unearthing my tap root stemming shame,
and wrapped my rink of wrath in radiance
exchanging Your right light for my blame.

Taking my hand into Your own,
You slipped on me Your promise ring's value,
and sealed my soul with priceless purity
to be Your white-gowned diamond dew.

You rescued me from my rot's realm,
to parks of peace with my Creator,
there grafting in my wild branch
to cling Your heavenly equator.

Suckling from Your nature's source,
I spiral up springtime's staircase,
as Your sure cross upholds my fall
with triumph's trellising embrace.

You put a new spin on my lunar life
to orbit 'round free skies, a glowing dove,
where forever I'll abideth in,
Your endless evergreen vine's love.

Giving off no light my pocked-rock owns,
I only shine of what Your grace to me does gleam,
just a reflection of Your lamp's love,
set aglow under Your sovereignty's sunbeam.

Jewel of Fire, Crowned Corona,
immune to dark side's kryptonite,
though dusk surrounds, You reign all, super-strobed
to starry host my garden's candlelight.

I am Your harvest's new moonflower,
unfolding my heart to touch midday,
adopted in Your morning's glory family,
to grow amidst Your mercy's milky way.

<u>sea seductress.</u>

Swirling tinseled eddies gleamed
charmed with gems of melted peridot,
like an enchanted sea seductress
bewitched by evil's undertow.

With my heated soles slow-burning,
I wet my feet among her tide,
courting shoreline's beguiling quicksand
when my digging heels began to slide.

Lured by her sky-dyed bedroom eyes
that danced between green's shiny-sheeted glare,
my baited-breath opened it's mouth
swallowing fishhook's sinker of despair.

Caught inside her breaker's surf,
I full-throated a futile whitewashed plea,
but my dueling desire was firmly bridled
reigned by my temptress' accosting sea.

Collected captive like the sand,
I whirled 'round her world incessantly,
as her riptide reeled me in
to drift her acquiescently.

Sounding down, I took her deeper,
without my will's fight to impede,
I made her barb my servant's master,
and her line's deceit my lead.

Chained to my anchoring addiction,
I quickly plunged towards bottom's floor,
hearing my heavy weighted wantonness
slam down my keeper's deathtrap door.

Locked up by her lording latch,
I became her plundered treasure chest,
pillaged by impassioned pirates
while in the arms of her arrest.

Like a harborless heart's holocaust,
tattooed with enemy's hate crimes,
I survived, her prison camper
detained in fields of loaded mines.
Gangplanks blindfolded my eyes,
keeping my mind masked in the dark,
as I awaited execution
inside my chamber's shipwrecked ark.

Held hostage in her hell's hive,
under my queen bee's full command,
I wedged my faith through slivered portholes
fingering my cemetery sand.

Cracks of hope came hatching promise
through my eggshell fallen from it's nest,
to my dim fathoms where Your grace appeared
and morn's mercy did manifest.

Your torch of truth had touched me,
sunlighting my sin, then unsurrendered,
when helplessly, my soul cried out
for my Life Guard and breath extender.

Sought out within my turbulence,
I felt Your calm quiet my storm,
swept by Your saving swells of sovereignty
into Your current safe and warm.

Onto Your wide-armed beach, You pulled me,
when I had no more to invest,
gathering my driftwood's scattered remnant
You answered my wracked ruin's request.

Now on the shore land of the living,
upon my soul's salvation's Rock,
once drowned, now saved, I'll ever praise,
Your cape's coastline, I'll choose to walk.

For far-reaching was Your rescue
when Your might's mercy did descend,
to be my Life Preserving Hero,
assuring me in You I can depend.

<u>**crusader.**</u>

When I was four, I dressed like batman.
Now I'm a crusader for the Lord
having confessed my false identity
to gain my King's righteous reward.

I remember being sure back then,
someday I'd fly like Superman,
I used to flap my little arms so hard
that they would bruise me as I ran.

One day, caped in my own confidence,
while puffing out the "S" marked on my chest,
I crawled high atop my houses roof'
and bound out on my quest.

Looking back upon that painful day,
I regret I didn't know God's truth,
that never would I be a super hero
by changing clothes inside a booth.

That "S" I once thought brought me strength,
I know better now stamped Satan's grin,
because when I tried to steel God's glory
my holey t-shirt stood for sin.

At age 12, I liked pretending
Jesus was my spiritual high chief,
but He was no more than a legend
for my tribe's rain dancing belief.

By 17, I was quite competitive.
I played school sports to win a star.
I was the captain of the varsity.
I thought my efforts would go far.

Then off to college to visit my wild side,
and serve my flesh it's wanton sweets,
where I masqueraded as the good witch
so my trick's reaped for me treats.

Next, came my Indiana Jane stage
adventuring around God's globe,
I trekked the Himalayan mountains
and toured Burma in a robe.

I ran with bulls through streets of Spain,
explored Egyptian Pyramids.
I picnicked at the Taj Mahal
and fed the mouths of hungry kids.

Flying back home one year later,
my senses quaked with culture shock,
for my eyes had seen the tragedy
I now knew lived around the block.

Yet still knowing other's anguished,
I hunted down myself a job.
I threw my nose ring in the top drawer,
and joined the corporate yuppie mob.

My business means afforded me
a prestigious pay-checked quilt
to cover up my sickened soul
under a sham to hide my guilt.

I learned that status stating symbols
could offer nothing to my soul.
I had prestige, profit, and power,
yet, never once did I feel whole.

Surely relationships must be the way
to fill my unfulfilled heart's needs.
But I found out the hard way,
no one on earth could do that deed.

In my hot pursuit for happiness,
I'd been religious all along,
I'd based salvation on my goodness
unaware my requirement was wrong.

Then one night, my faith was challenged
with a prodding of my shallow Christian view,
that's when God began to let me see
His divine reality was true.

The next three days I fought a battle,
within my own minds tug-of-war,
hearing my soul's enemy shout,
"It's your imagination, nothing more!"

Satan promised me convincingly,
"God's truth for you is wrong,"
but God held me in His faithful hands
keeping my confused spirit strong.

Quickly God invited me to honor
my mom's birthday request,
to join her and my father at church,
I would be their unsuspecting guest.

Though my head had heard before
how Christ gave His life for me,
that Sunday morning my heart trusted
to receive His Life eternally.

Quietly confessing of my sinfulness,
thankful salvation was to me unpriced,
that day I gave away my wretchedness
to my precious Savior, Jesus Christ!

As heaven opened up attentively,
Holy Hands embraced my prayer,
making a way for me, a sinner,
to become His child, Christ's co-heir.

Now every single day since then,
my once empty place gives this reply,
"Thank You for setting my heart free
from Satan's mind deceiving lie!"

Dizzy.
The Trouble-Talking Tornado

I used to know a boy named Dizzy.
I called him Dizzy Trouble Talk
because his worried words and thoughts
would wind him up as he would walk.

Round and round his trouble talking
turned him with a torque
until his twisted neck unwound
sending him flying like a cork.

Then off would reel young Dizzy
side-winding north, south, east, and west,
like a tail spinning tornado
without a single moment's rest.

Dizzy's mind was always busy
with troubled thoughts instead of peace
that's why his ever-swiveling hair-tossed head
never seemed to cease.

Poor very Dizzy Trouble Talk
how like a top that boy would twirl
flailing his arms into a frenzy
as he whipped wildly with a whirl.

One day I chased that Dizzy down,
and as his pinwheel parts blew south,
I got just close enough to hear
his winded words blow from his mouth.

Without wasting any time,
I asked him straight without delaying,
"Won't you please stop to give some thought
to all this nonsense you are saying?"

"All your double-minded trouble talk
has trained your brain to become dizzy.
Aren't your worried words and thoughts
what put your innards in a tizzy?"

Thinking through my questions
must have revved up Dizzy higher
because his turbo shoes took off
leaving a trail of blazing fire.

Bolting brightly through the park,
Dizzy dashed across the lawn
whizzing westbound with a *WHOOOSH*
just as the sprinkler heads turned on!

Then like a stopped mop in a carwash
Dizzy's drenched do droop down flat
his limp locks lapped around his face
down to the grass which he now sat.

In almost no time, sparks came flying
from his ears amidst the drizzle
before a crowd gathered to watch
as Dizzy fizzled with a sizzle!

Sobered to his senses
by the short-circuiting rain,
Dizzy shook his muddled mind
until his blurry brain was sane.

With a soft heart, I stepped towards him
and as my slushing sneakers neared,
his wet tresses tilted toward me
and his flush face reappeared.

Welcomed by the woundedness
his teary blue eyes cried,
I stretched my loving arm around him
and I sat down by his side.

He said,
"I understand now that my thoughts and words
can stir me up or make me still.
My mind and body work together
like a mood moving windmill."

"Now when troubling thoughts come near
I'm going to cast away those cares,
and choose to think of happy things
with thankfulness and trusting prayers."

"I've traded in my trouble talk
for winning words, I'll choose to say,
so that my spiraled steps go straight
and I can walk a different way."

Now I can't call my wise friend Dizzy
since worried words he overcame.
I'll have to think of a replacement
for his old trouble talking name.

Singleness Sings

"And I pray that you,
being rooted and grounded in love,
may have power, together with the saints,
to grasp how wide and long
and high and deep is the love of Christ,
and to know this love that surpasses knowledge —
that you may be filled to the measure
of all the fullness of God."

- Ephesians 3:17-19

<u>**formula one.**</u>

I've chosen not
the marriage mess,
not puppeted,
but prophetess.

Called not to die
domesticated,
but bought to live
life liberated!

Making music
with my Maker,
not all consumed
by man's dream taker.

To win some souls
that might be lost.
I've counted up
my choice's cost.

I did the math.
I summed it up.
I'd rather sip
my single's cup.

I've seen suburban
SUV's
filled with their kids
and dog degrees.

With skis on top
and bikes on back
their four-wheeled
social status-ed rack.

But I like my soul's
speedway's route,
for my fine-tuned
car's roundabout.

An Indy car
with just one seat.
Formula 1!
I am complete!

More streamlined
than an SUV
without much baggage
slowing me.

Ride unencumbered,
full-throttled thrill,
has trumped, for me,
mommy's mobile.

So pity not
my single state.
My drive's Divine
without a mate!

The curves I take
are from cloud 9
because I left
a spouse behind!

tandem bike.

I saw a couple cross a road
riding tandem on a bike.
Both of them held handlebars
and feet pedaled alike.

The only difference was the man
held handlebars in front to steer
while his wife's bars never moved
as she sat stiffly in the rear.

I decided on that summer's day,
I'd never be the trailing tail
riding tandem in the backseat
of solo-steering male!

<u>widow's wings.</u>

You found me among ruins
burying bones in broken rooms.
I was a vulture in a valley
eating dead flesh out of tombs.

My soul was just a scavenger
amid scorched lands lonely waste.
My tears, ten rushing rivers
filled with a sorrow-salted taste.

I was a sister to the jackals,
a companion known by owls.
My heart, an echoed haunt
of wounded wails and hurting howls.

Sadness moved to madness.
Revenge ripened rage.
Bitterness built bars
for my unforgiveness cage.

Then abandoned in my ashes,
sifting through shards of shattered dreams,
You rescued me from blackbird's night,
my songbird's Savior Who redeems!

You raised me up out from the wreckage
of my mourning dove's dark heart
to sing a rousing resurrection
with widow's wings, You did impart!

A bird of prey, I am no longer,
but now, set free, a bird of prayer!
You are my spirit's Wind Uplifter
thrusting me weightless in the air!

<u>not a hornblower.</u>

I'm so glad Aretha Franklin
embraced her gift when she was born,
and didn't sacrifice her singing
for a career blowing a horn.

What if our folksy Joni Mitchell
had traded singing for a sax?
The world would still be at a loss
without her sweet songbird's sound tracks.

I'm glad Miss Whitney Houston
wasn't forced to play a flute
fulfilling her legend's lesser destiny
for which no one would give a hoot.

What if Stevie Nicks was tempted
to play a long sliding trombone?
We would have never heard the brilliance
of her gypsy's sultry tone.

What if Woodstock's Janis Joplin
had bought a brass horn for her lips?
We would have never been invited on
her passion's pleasure trips.

Let's not mute Mariah's music box,
or block Beyoncé's breath.
Let's not smother Streisand's song
putting her resonance to death.

Not all women are hornblowers.
Some are born and blessed to sing,
so leave your bugles at the backdoor
and let a sister's freedom ring!

<u>the Jerry McGuire gospel.</u>

According to McGuire's gospel
Jerry has requirements to meet,
that I must wed my better half
to be entirely complete.

Without a man, I'm just "half Christian,"
unmarried – I'm rated "second-class,"
without a ring on my left finger,
I'm deemed a worthless lonely lass.

But I won't drink this culture's Kool-Aid
served to intoxicate my mind
with a false gospel Jerry preaches
that through a man I am defined.

Even the Church has bought this madness
of Satan's matrimony lie,
that a lone woman can't be whole
without a status-stamping guy.

McGuire's marriage is an idol –
his mind's molten golden calf,
a fleshly union of two fractions,
both made whole through their lost half.

But my degree is not my M.R.S.
or from a brass ring in a game,
but in Christ, my worth is found
through His death, God's love did claim!

Christ's Gospel holds the real Truth -
that in Him I am complete!
I've not been banished from the kingdom
of God's heavenly elite.

I am My Prince's cherished princess!
The Cinderella of His story!
He is my spirit's treasure trove,
God's mystery, my hope of glory!

www.ingramcontent.com/pod-product-compliance
Lightning Source LLC
Chambersburg PA
CBHW061734050726
47598CB00002B/475